THE AI CUSTOMER ACQUISITION PLAYBOOK

How to Attract, Nurture & Convert Customers at Scale

BY DR. JEROME JOSEPH

GLOBAL BRAND THOUGHT LEADER & AI STRATEGIST

INDIA • SINGAPORE • MALAYSIA

Copyright © Dr. Jerome Joseph 2025
All Rights Reserved.

ISBN
Paperback 979-8-89961-553-5
Hardcase 979-8-89984-278-8

CONTENTS

In the age of AI, it's not about who has the most tools — it's about who knows how to use them to build trust, connection, and unstoppable growth.

Welcome to the New Age of Customer Growth

HOW A FRUSTRATED ENTREPRENEUR ALMOST GAVE UP — UNTIL AI CHANGED EVERYTHING

A few months ago, I was having coffee with an entrepreneur I'd previously coached — let's call him Daniel. Daniel runs a mid-sized consulting business. Smart, experienced, and driven. But when it came to growing his customer base, he was frustrated.

"Jerome," he told me, *"I'm spending hours writing content, trying to engage my audience, building funnels... but nothing's working. The content feels generic. It's exhausting. And honestly, I feel like I'm shouting into the void."*

Daniel had tried everything:
- Posting on social media every day
- Writing email newsletters
- Running ads
- Experimenting with AI writing tools — but the output felt robotic, soulless, and disconnected

He was busy, but not productive.
Visible, but not converting.
Present online, but not profitable.
And Daniel isn't alone.

Over the past year, I've worked with entrepreneurs, executives, and business owners facing the same struggle: They jumped on the AI bandwagon—only to get overwhelmed, confused, and burnt out.

The Problem Isn't AI — It's How You Use It

The digital landscape has changed forever. We no longer live in a world where the loudest brand wins.
Today, the smartest, fastest, and most strategic brands dominate.

Artificial Intelligence is the most powerful business growth accelerator of our time.

But here's the uncomfortable truth:

AI doesn't make you money.
What you do with AI does.

Without a system, without a strategy, without brand clarity — AI will only amplify the confusion in your business.

That's why I created this playbook.

The AI Customer Acquisition Playbook™
How to Attract, Nurture & Convert Customers at Scale

This is not another "how-to" guide filled with complicated tech jargon, empty promises, or gimmicky hacks.

It is a **proven, ethical, and scalable system** designed to help you:
- Use AI to get customers FAST
- Amplify your unique voice without sounding generic
- Automate your marketing flow without losing authenticity
- And most importantly — build trust, credibility, and authority at scale

What's Inside This Playbook

This isn't just information — it's a tactical, actionable system. In the pages ahead, you'll discover:

SECTION 1 : WHY MOST PEOPLE FAIL WITH AI (AND HOW YOU CAN SUCCEED)

Learn the common mistakes businesses make when using AI—and how you can avoid them to stay ahead of the curve.

SECTION 2 : HOW TO MAKE AI WORK FOR YOU (THE RIGHT WAY)

Get a step-by-step framework to use AI strategically and effectively for rapid customer acquisition.

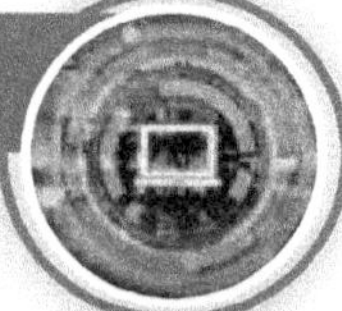

SECTION 3 : THE AI CUSTOMER ACQUISITION PLAYBOOK™

Your complete, tactical guide — with ready-to-use prompts, templates, and exercises to help you create persuasive content, nurture relationships, and drive conversions.

SECTION 4 : AUTOMATE & SCALE – BUILDING YOUR AI CUSTOMER ACQUISITION ENGINE

Discover how to automate your entire customer acquisition process using AI-powered systems — so you can scale without burning out.

SECTION 5 : THE AI SALES CONVERSION BLUEPRINT

Master the structure, psychology, and execution of writing high-converting sales copy, sales pages, and offers using AI — without sounding robotic.

SECTION 6 : NEXT STEPS – SCALING, SUSTAINING & MASTERING YOUR AI CUSTOMER ACQUISITION SYSTEM

You'll walk away with a clear, advanced roadmap to help you grow, sustain, and master your AI-driven customer acquisition engine—plus tools, programs, and bonus resources.

Your Competitive Edge Starts Here

By the end of this playbook, you won't just know how to "use AI."
You'll have a clear, scalable, and ethical system to Attract, Nurture & Convert Customers at Scale.

You'll move beyond content creation — and start building a real, automated, and sustainable customer acquisition machine.

**So if you're ready to stop guessing and start growing...
Turn the page.
Your AI-powered growth system starts now.**

Technology amplifies the person who wields it. AI will not fix your business — **but** strategy, clarity, and intention will.

WHY MOST PEOPLE FAIL WITH AI
(AND HOW YOU CAN SUCCEED)

THE BIG LIE ABOUT AI IN MARKETING

We are living through the noisiest era of business marketing in history. Every day, you are bombarded with headlines promising:

> *"AI will make you millions overnight!"*
> *"Automate your sales while you sleep!"*
> *"One-click customers at zero cost!"*

And this is exactly why so many people are getting it wrong.

Let me be clear right from the start: AI will not save your business. It will only amplify what's already there — whether it's clear, cluttered, or completely chaotic.

I've worked with hundreds of entrepreneurs, executives, and sales professionals over the last two years as AI exploded into the mainstream. Most of them made the same mistake:

They treated AI like a vending machine.

Press a button -> Get customers

Push a prompt -> Watch the money roll in.

But business doesn't work like that. And neither does AI.

What most people don't realise is this:

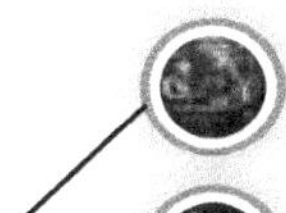
AI is not the strategy.

AI is the vehicle.

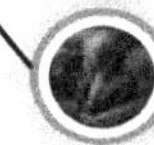
You are the driver.

THE 3 FATAL MISTAKES MOST PEOPLE MAKE WITH AI

 **MISTAKE #1: CONFUSING TOOLS WITH STRATEGY**

The biggest myth around AI is that the tool itself is the solution. People assume that by having access to the latest AI platform — whether it's ChatGPT, Jasper, Claude, Grok, or any other — they've automatically gained an advantage.

But let me ask you: If you bought the world's best camera today, would that instantly make you a world-class photographer?
Of course not.
You would still need:

 **The right mindset**

 **An understanding of light, composition, and storytelling**

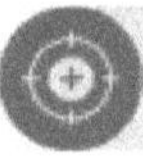 **A clear purpose for every shot you take**

AI is no different.
It is a powerful, game-changing tool.
But without a clear strategy, without customer insight, without brand positioning—all you'll get is beautifully written nonsense that doesn't move the needle.
What To Do Instead: You must start with absolute clarity:

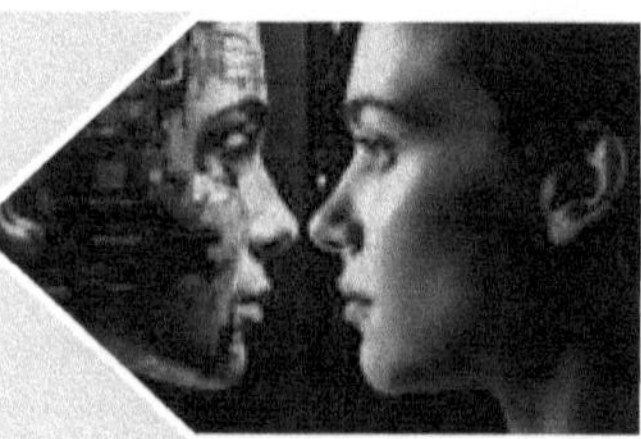

- **Who exactly is my target audience?**
- **What is their deepest pain point, frustration, or desire?**
- **What unique solution do I bring to the table?**

AI will only multiply the clarity you bring to the table.
If you're unclear, AI will simply help you confuse more people, faster.

THE 3 FATAL MISTAKES MOST PEOPLE MAKE WITH AI

 **MISTAKE #2: USING WEAK, VAGUE, OR LAZY PROMPTS**

AI only gives you what you ask for.

And here's where most users go wrong: They feed AI shallow, generic, or poorly-structured prompts — and then complain that the output is average or robotic.

Here's an example of a bad prompt: *"Write me an email to get customers."* That's like walking into a Michelin-star restaurant and saying: *"Cook me food."*

You'll get something on your plate, sure.

But will it satisfy you? Will it wow you? Will it convert?

No.

Because vague inputs = vague outcomes.

What To Do Instead: You need to give AI clear, structured, objective-driven prompts — just like you would brief a professional copywriter.

For example:
"Write me a persuasive email for first-time entrepreneurs aged 25-35, explaining how our digital marketing masterclass can help them get their first 10 clients in 30 days. Use a friendly, professional tone and include a clear call-to-action."

When you control the inputs, you control the outcome.

Prompting is an art and a strategy — and you'll master this in the next section.

THE 3 FATAL MISTAKES MOST PEOPLE MAKE WITH AI

 **MISTAKE #3: FORGETTING THE HUMAN CONNECTION**

Here's something I need you to remember:
Customers don't buy from AI.
They buy from brands they trust.
They buy from people who understand them.
They buy from businesses that connect with them emotionally.
Too many people get seduced by the speed and scale of AI.
They automate everything, remove human touch, and end up with beautifully worded content that nobody reads—and nobody buys from.
The result?
A hollow, mechanical brand voice that pushes people away instead of pulling them in.

What To Do Instead: Use AI to do the heavy lifting — but **always infuse your content with:**

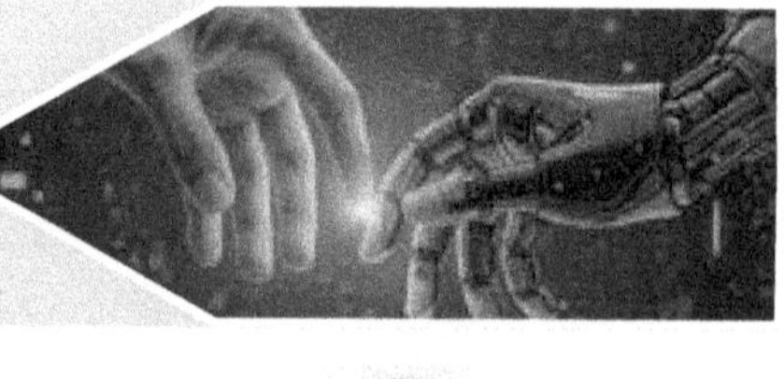

- **Your brand values**
- **A clear call-to-action**
- **Empathy, relevance, and clarity**

AI is your assistant, not your replacement.
You are the connection.

THE HIDDEN COST OF GETTING AI WRONG

Let me share something you won't read in the AI hype headlines:

When you misuse AI, the damage goes beyond bad content.

You're damaging your brand equity.

You're eroding trust.

You're creating noise, not value.

Poorly written, irrelevant, or generic AI content does three dangerous things:

1. REDUCES TRUST

Your audience can instantly sense automated junk

2. HURTS YOUR CREDIBILITY

You sound like every other brand chasing trends

3. DESTROYS LONG-TERM RELATIONSHIPS

No one builds loyalty with a robot

And in a digital world where your brand's currency is trust and authority, this is a price too high to pay.

WHY YOU'LL WIN
(WHEN OTHERS FAIL)

Most people will keep misusing AI. They'll chase shortcuts, pump out low-quality content, and wonder why they're not growing. But you're not most people.

By the time you finish this playbook, you'll know:

How to strategically use AI to attract, nurture, and convert customers

How to integrate AI into your brand voice and business system

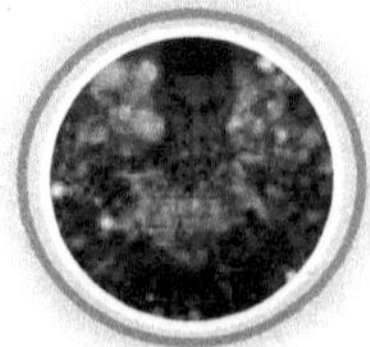

How to ethically automate without losing the human connection

How to build a sustainable, scalable AI-powered customer acquisition engine

You will be in the 1% who uses AI not as a gimmick — but as a growth engine.

ACTION STEP: BUILD BRAND CLARITY BEFORE YOU AUTOMATE

Before you move to Section 2, take five minutes to answer these three powerful questions:

1. What is the single most valuable result I offer my customers?
(Example: Help small businesses grow their customer base fast.)

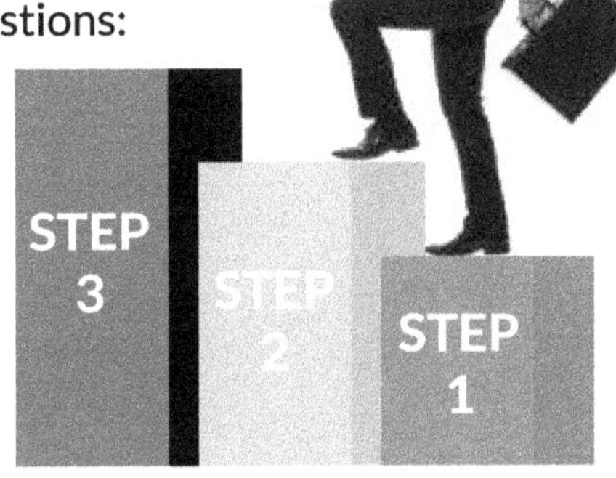

____

____

____

____

____

2. What makes my voice, style, and brand different from others in my industry? (Example: Direct, no-nonsense, actionable.)

____

____

____

____

3. Who exactly do I want to reach with my content?
Be specific. Age, profession, location, challenges, desires.

____

____

____

____

Write them down.
You'll use these answers to craft laser-targeted AI prompts in the next section.

AI is not the magic — your system is the magic. When you combine human strategy with machine speed, you become unstoppable

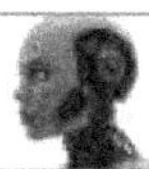

HOW TO MAKE AI WORK FOR YOU
(THE RIGHT WAY)

THE DIFFERENCE BETWEEN AI USERS AND AI WINNERS

There are two types of people in this AI-driven business landscape:

THE AI USERS

These are the masses who treat AI like a vending machine.
They punch in a vague prompt, grab the first piece of content it spits out, post it online, and wonder why their inbox is empty and their sales pipeline dry.

Their results?
Mediocre.
Forgettable.
Unscalable.

THE AI WINNERS

These are the select few who approach AI differently.
They don't treat it as a toy — they treat it as a tool, a system, and a strategic business asset.

They:
- **Systemise their content creation**
- **Humanise their messaging**
- **Scale their marketing machine**
- **And most importantly — drive real business growth**

This section is designed to help you become one of them.

Because the truth is:
AI will not automatically create customers for you.
But when used strategically, it will help you attract, nurture, and convert customers at scale — faster than ever before.

THE A.I. CUSTOMER ACQUISITION SYSTEM™

To help you make AI work for you the right way, I've developed a simple, powerful 4-step system.

This is the exact process I teach in my workshops, keynotes, and to private clients — designed to make AI an integral, profitable part of your customer acquisition strategy.

The 4 Steps:

1 CLARITY BEFORE TECHNOLOGY

2 MASTER THE ART OF PROMPT ENGINEERING

3 TRAIN AI TO SOUND LIKE YOU

4 BUILD YOUR AI-POWERED CUSTOMER ACQUISITION FUNNEL

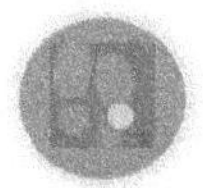

STEP 1: **CLARITY BEFORE TECHNOLOGY**

Here's where 90% of people fail.

They get excited by the AI tools.
They jump in, start prompting, generating content — but they have no clarity about what they actually want to achieve.

AI without clarity is like giving a sports car to someone who doesn't know where they're going.
Fast — but directionless.

What You Must Be Clear On:

Ask Yourself:

1. **What specific outcome do I want from this content?**
   (Lead generation? Sales? Brand awareness? Nurturing?)

2. **Who is my audience?**
   Be precise: Age, profession, location, keyfrustrations, desires.

3. **What specific action do I want them to take after consuming this content?**
   (Book a call? Download a guide? Make a purchase?)

Without these answers, your prompts will be weak and your results average.

Example:
- **Weak Prompt** *"Write me a sales email."*
- **Strategic Prompt** *"Write me a persuasive email to small business owners aged 30-45 who want to grow their sales but struggle with digital marketing. The email should introduce our free AI Customer Growth Webinar, highlight three key benefits, and end with a clear call-to-action."*

That difference is everything.
- **Clear intention = Stronger, more profitable AI output.**

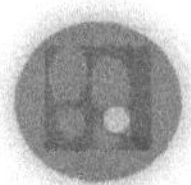

STEP 2: **MASTER THE ART OF PROMPT ENGINEERING**

Your AI output is only as good as your input.
The prompt is everything.

Think of prompting as giving AI a creative brief — exactly like you would brief a professional copywriter, content strategist, or marketing consultant.

The 5-Point Prompt Formula™

Every prompt you give AI should include these five elements:

1. Role – Who should AI act as?
(Example: "Act as an experienced sales copywriter with expertise in digital marketing.")

2. Objective – What is the primary goal of the content?
(Example: "To write an email sequence that converts leads into customers.")

3. Audience – Who is the target reader?
(Example: "Corporate leaders in the financial services sector.")

4.Context – Provide background, relevant information, tone, and style.
(Example: "This is part of a customer acquisition funnel. The tone should be professional, friendly, and direct.")

5. Action – What do you want the reader to do?
(Example: "Click the link to book a discovery call.")

Example:
"Act as a digital marketing strategist. Write a LinkedIn post for financial advisors who want to use AI to grow their customer base. Keep it professional, engaging, and end with a clear call to action to download our free AI Customer Growth Checklist."

When you master the art of prompting, you unlock AI's full potential — and your content will improve overnight.

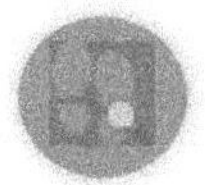

STEP 3: **TRAIN AI TO SOUND LIKE YOU**

Here's the uncomfortable truth most marketers won't tell you: If your AI content sounds generic, robotic, or boring — it's not AI's fault. It's yours.
Because you haven't taught AI how to sound like you.

Your audience wants to connect with your voice, your values, and your personality.
That's why training AI to adopt your brand voice is essential.

How To Train AI On Your Brand Voice:

1. Provide Sample Content:
Share 2–3 pages of your best-performing emails, articles, or social posts.

2. Give Clear Instructions:
Prompt AI to study your content:
"Read every word of the sample content. Learn my style, tone, sentence structure, and word choice. Do not use the content itself. Use it only to learn how I write."

3.Refine The Output:
Once AI produces content, guide it:
- *"Make it more conversational."*
- *"Add a clear call-to-action."*
- *"Simplify the sentences."*
- *"Make it sound like I'm speaking directly to the reader."*

Pro Tip:
Create a reusable "Brand Voice Template" prompt: *"Here's my brand voice: Direct, professional, conversational, with a touch of humour. Always focus on value and practical advice. No jargon. No fluff. Write everything in this voice."*

When you do this, your AI-generated content won't just sound good — it will sound like you.

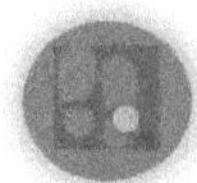

STEP 4: BUILD YOUR AI-POWERED CUSTOMER ACQUISITION FUNNEL

This is where most people get it wrong.

They use AI to create one post, one email, one random piece of content at a time.

That's not how you win customers.

That's how you stay busy without results.

You need to build a clear, strategic Customer Acquisition Funnel — powered by AI, but designed by you.

The 3 Stages of Your Funnel:

1. Attract (Awareness Content)

Your goal is to get noticed, educate, and engage. Use AI to generate:

- Blog articles
- Social media posts
- Lead magnets (guides, checklists, templates)

Prompt Example:

"Create a list of 10 LinkedIn post ideas for financial planners who want to use AI to grow their client base."

2. Engage (Connection Content)

Your goal is to nurture, build trust, and demonstrate authority. Use AI to help you craft:

- Email newsletters
- Webinar invitations
- Educational email sequences
- Value-packed social content

Prompt Example:

"Write a 5-part email nurture sequence for financial advisors who downloaded our 'AI Growth Checklist.' Include valuable tips and end each email with a call-to-action to book a discovery call."

3. Convert (Sales Content)

This is where you invite people to take action. Use AI to write:

- Sales pages
- Offer emails
- Webinar scripts
- Call-to-action content

Prompt Example:

"Write a persuasive sales email inviting entrepreneurs to join our 'AI Customer Acquisition Bootcamp.' Highlight the key benefits, include a limited-time bonus, and end with a clear call-to-action."

CASE STUDY: TRIPLING LEADS IN 30 DAYS

Let me show you what this looks like in action.

One of my clients, a financial advisor in Singapore, used this exact system.
He wasn't a copywriter. He wasn't tech-savvy.
But he followed these four steps:

- He got clear on his audience: Young professionals aged 25–35
- He used my Prompt Formula to build a structured nurture sequence
- He trained AI on his voice and personal story
- He built a simple, clear customer acquisition funnel

The result?
In just 30 days:

- His email list grew by 300%
- He booked 17 discovery calls
- He closed 6 new clients
- His pipeline remained consistently full without him manually creating every piece of content

Not because AI is magic.
But because he used AI the right way — strategically, ethically, and systematically.

ACTION STEP: BUILD YOUR AI PROMPT LIBRARY

Before moving to the next section, take your first step toward becoming an AI Winner.

Start your AI Prompt Library: Create 5–10 well-structured, reusable prompts tailored to your audience, offer, and brand voice.

Examples:
1. Write a LinkedIn post for [audience] about [topic] with a call-to-action to [desired action].
2. Write a nurturing email for people who downloaded [lead magnet] to invite them to book a consultation.
3. Write a blog outline addressing [audience challenge] for [target audience].
4. Write a persuasive email promoting our [product/service].
5. Create a list of 10 content ideas for [target audience] about [topic].

This is how you stop being an average AI user — and start building an AI-powered customer acquisition engine.

Success is not built on random content. It's built on systems, strategy, and a clear path that turns strangers into customers — at scale

THE A.I. CUSTOMER ACQUISITION PLAYBOOK™

FROM THEORY TO EXECUTION – YOUR AI CUSTOMER GROWTH ENGINE

You now understand the mindset and strategy behind using AI effectively. You've seen why most people fail and how you can avoid their mistakes.

Now it's time to move beyond strategy and step into execution.

This section is your tactical playbook — a proven, step-by-step system to help you deploy AI effectively and turn it into a customer acquisition machine.

If you follow this playbook and apply what you learn, you'll be able to produce high-quality, persuasive, brand-aligned content in minutes — not weeks — without sacrificing your voice or authenticity.

What You'll Learn in This Section

- How to turn boring, underperforming content into powerful, brand-building assets
- How to train AI to adopt your brand
- voice and writing style
- How to instantly generate audience-ready, high-converting marketing content
- How to create persuasive, objective-driven content that drives results
- How to structure a complete sales letter, lead magnet, or campaign using AI

PART A: REWRITE & AMPLIFY — TRANSFORM DULL CONTENT INTO BRAND-DRIVING CONTENT

Most businesses already have content lying around — old articles, forgotten email drafts, stale brochures, blog posts that never performed. The fastest way to start winning with AI is not to reinvent the wheel — but to improve what you already have.

The Rewrite System

Here's how to make AI your elite content editor:

STEP 1: **Feed AI Your Existing Content**

Prompt: *"I'm going to paste an article below. Don't write anything yet. Just read it, understand the key points, and tell me when you're ready."* [Paste content]

STEP 2: **Identify The Gold**

Prompt: *"What are the most compelling points in this article? Identify the strongest hooks, key benefits, and unique angles."*

STEP 3: **Improve The Structure**

Prompt: *"Give me a stronger, clearer outline of this content, focusing on the most persuasive parts and adding clear calls-to-action."*

STEP 4: **ReWrite & Amplify**

Prompt: *"Now rewrite the entire article based on this outline. Keep it professional, conversational, and engaging. Ensure it's written for [target audience]. Make it concise, punchy, and persuasive."*

Optional Enhancements:

- "Add a stronger opening and closing."
- "Use shorter sentences."
- "Make it sound like a premium brand copywriter wrote this."

Outcome:

You'll end up with professional, polished, and powerful content — ready to engage and convert.

PART B: THE VOICE ENGINE — TRAIN AI TO WRITE LIKE YOU

The biggest mistake business owners make with AI is allowing it to sound like... well, an AI.

Your audience doesn't buy from a robot.

They buy from YOU.

Your voice, your values, your brand personality.

Here's how to make AI sound exactly like you:

The Voice Calibration Method

STEP 1: **Select Your Best Content**

Choose 2–3 of your best-performing emails, articles, or social media posts.

STEP 2: **Feed AI Your Samples**

Prompt: *"Here's a sample of my writing. Study it carefully and learn my style, tone, sentence structure, and word choice. Do not use the content itself. Only use it to understand how I communicate."*
[Paste samples]

STEP 3: **Test & Refine**

Prompt: *"Now write a LinkedIn post for [target audience] about [topic] in my exact writing style. Keep it friendly, professional, and engaging."*

Optional Enhancements:

- "Make it more conversational."
- "Simplify the language to a sixth-grade reading level."
- "Use shorter sentences and punchier language."

Outcome:

You'll have AI-generated content that sounds like it was written by you, keeping your brand voice consistent at scale.

PART C: INSTANT CONTENT BUILDER — AI-GENERATED, AUDIENCE-READY CONTENT

There will be times when you need fresh content — fast.
Instead of staring at a blank page, use AI to generate quality content instantly.

Your Essential Content Prompts

Social Media Content Prompt:

"Write a LinkedIn post for corporate leaders about how AI is transforming customer acquisition. Keep it professional, engaging, and end with a question to spark discussion."

Lead Magnet Email Prompt:

"Write an email to professionals aged 30–45, inviting them to download our free guide on 'How to Use AI for Rapid Business Growth.' Make it friendly, persuasive, and end with a clear call-to-action."

Sales Page Prompt:

"Write a sales page for our 2-hour online masterclass, 'AI-Powered Customer Growth.' Highlight the key benefits, who it's for, and include a clear call-to-action."

Webinar Invitation Prompt:

"Write a professional, engaging email inviting entrepreneurs to attend our free webinar on using AI to grow their business. Include three key benefits of attending."

Content Calendar Prompt:

"Create a 1-month content calendar for LinkedIn posts targeting financial advisors who want to use AI to acquire more customers."

Pro Tip:

You can use these templates as-is or fine-tune them with audience-specific details, tone adjustments, and clear objectives.
80% of the work will be done in minutes.

PART D: THE INFLUENCE FRAMEWORK — CREATE CONTENT THAT CONVERTS

Here's why most AI-generated content fails:

It's informational, but not influential.

It speaks, but doesn't sell.

It educates, but doesn't persuade.

Your content must do four things:

1. **Convince** — Show your audience why your solution matters
2. **Build Authority** — Position you as the expert
3. **Educate** — Add value without giving everything away
4. **Drive Action** — Get your audience to take the next step

The Objective-Based Prompt Formula

Prompt: *"I need help creating [type of content]. The audience is [target market] who want [specific result]. The objective is threefold:

1. Convince them that [solution] will help them achieve their desired result.
2. Position me as the expert and make them want to learn more from me.
3. Provide them with actionable tips they can use immediately. End with a clear call-to-action."*

Use this formula for:

- Emails
- Blog posts
- Social media content
- Sales pages
- Lead magnets

This is how you shift from content creator -> to customer magnet.

PART E: THE A.I. SALES LETTER BLUEPRINT — FROM ZERO TO CUSTOMER-READY COPY

For major campaigns, lead magnets, or product launches, you'll need long-form sales content.

Here's how to build it quickly and effectively with AI:

The 5 Key Sales Letter Questions

1. **What's the Problem?**
   The biggest frustration or desire of your audience.

2. **What's the Promise?**
   The specific result you're offering.

3. **What's the Proof?**
   Why should they trust you? (Testimonials, data, credentials)

4. **What's the Process?**
   How does your solution work?

5. **What's the Offer?**
   What do they get? Include price, bonuses, and guarantee.

Prompt Example:

"Here's the information about my offer (paste answers to the five questions). Write a direct response sales letter based on this, using professional, persuasive copy targeted at [audience]."

Once AI produces the draft, apply the Rewrite System (from Part A) to refine the tone, flow, and emotional impact.

YOUR AI EXECUTION CHECKLIST

Before moving to Section 4, make sure you've completed these steps:

1. Create your Brand Voice Template
2. Build your first 5–10 reusable, structured AI prompts
3. Train AI on your writing samples
4. Apply the Rewrite System to one piece of existing content
5. Use the Influence Framework to improve one piece of content
6. Draft a long-form sales letter using the Sales Letter Blueprint

When these elements are in place, you'll no longer be creating random content—you'll be operating a streamlined, systematic, AI-powered customer acquisition engine.

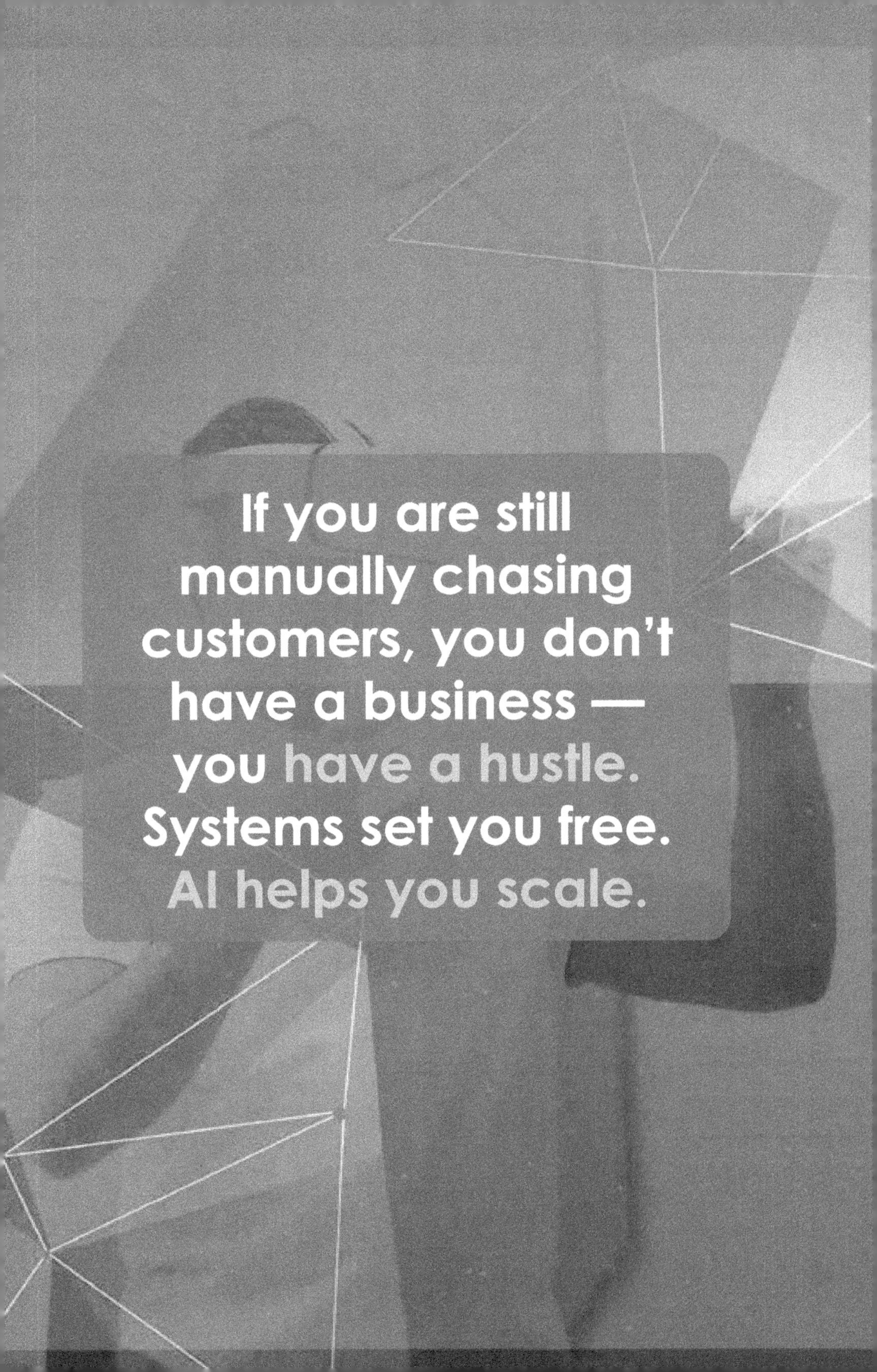

If you are still manually chasing customers, you don't have a business — you have a hustle. Systems set you free. AI helps you scale.

AUTOMATE & SCALE — BUILDING YOUR AI CUSTOMER ACQUISITION ENGINE

FROM CONTENT CREATION TO CUSTOMER FLOW

Let me share a truth that most AI "enthusiasts" won't tell you:

Content without structure is noise.

Content without a system is a waste.

Content without automation is a full-time job you didn't sign up for.

You can have the most engaging, AI-generated emails...

You can write sales letters that sound like a top copywriter crafted them...

You can post every day on LinkedIn, Instagram, and email your audience weekly...

But if there's no structure, no automation, no system — you will burn out, waste time, and lose opportunities.

This is where most people fail.

They focus on producing content but forget to build a system that turns that content into customers — predictably, repeatedly, and automatically.

In this section, I'll show you exactly how to convert your AI-powered content into a fully functional Customer Acquisition Engine™ — one that works even when you're not.

The 3 Pillars of AI Automation & Scaling

To automate and scale your customer acquisition process, you need three essential building blocks:

Pillar 1: Content Automation
Structure your content creation so you're not stuck in a daily content treadmill.

Pillar 2: Engagement Automation
Systemise how you nurture, educate, and build trust with leads — without manual effort.

Pillar 3: Conversion Automation
Create an automated sales funnel that turns leads into paying customers — predictably and consistently.

PILLAR 1: CONTENT AUTOMATION — THE VISIBILITY ENGINE

You now know how to create high-quality, brand-aligned content with AI. The next step is to ensure that content reaches your audience consistently without you lifting a finger daily.

The Content Calendar System

Strategy:
Batch-create content in advance using AI and schedule it to run automatically across your channels.

Prompt Example:
"Create a 4-week content calendar for LinkedIn and email, targeting small business owners aged 30–50 who want to use AI to grow their customer base. Include topics, objectives, and calls-to-action."

Execution Steps:
1. Generate Content Ideas & Drafts
   Use AI to create 4 weeks' worth of LinkedIn posts, email newsletters, and blog outlines.
2. Polish & Personalise
   Review the content. Add your personality, key brand messages, and fine-tune for relevance.
3. Automate Distribution
   Load your content into scheduling platforms like:
   - Buffer
   - Hootsuite
   - Later
   - LinkedIn's Native Scheduler
   - Email platforms like MailChimp or ActiveCampaign

Outcome:
You now have a month's worth of content running automatically — building visibility, credibility, and engagement without manual daily effort.

PILLAR 2: ENGAGEMENT AUTOMATION — THE NURTURE ENGINE

Content without engagement is noise.
Content without follow-up is wasted effort.

You need to turn casual readers into warm leads — and that requires a structured, automated nurture system.

The AI-Powered Email Nurture Sequence

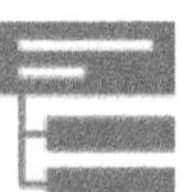

Structure:
- A 5–7 part email sequence designed to:
- Build trust
- Demonstrate expertise
- Offer value
- Lead prospects to take action

Typical Sequence Structure:
1. **Welcome Email:** Who you are, what you do, how you help
2. **Value Email #1:** Solve a small problem (Quick tip, free resource)
3. **Authority Email:** Share a client story, testimonial, or success result
4. **Value Email #2:** More helpful tips, insights, or behind-the-scenes
5. **Invitation Email:** Invite them to a webinar, discovery call, or consultation
6. **Sales Email:** Present your offer, highlight benefits, and include a clear call-to-action
7. **Reminder / Last Chance Email:** Create urgency, overcome objections

Prompt Example:
"Write a 7-part email nurture sequence for entrepreneurs aged 25–40 who want to learn how to use AI to grow their business. The sequence should educate, build trust, and invite them to attend our free 'AI Customer Acquisition Masterclass.'"

PILLAR 2: ENGAGEMENT AUTOMATION — THE NURTURE ENGINE

The AI-Powered Email Nurture Sequence

Execution Steps:
1. Create the sequence using AI
2. Review, personalise, and refine the copy
3. Load it into your email automation platform:
   - ActiveCampaign
   - MailChimp
   - ConvertKit
   - HubSpot
4. Trigger the sequence automatically when someone downloads your lead magnet or shows interest.

Outcome:

You now have an automated system that nurtures leads, builds relationships, and primes them to buy — while you sleep.

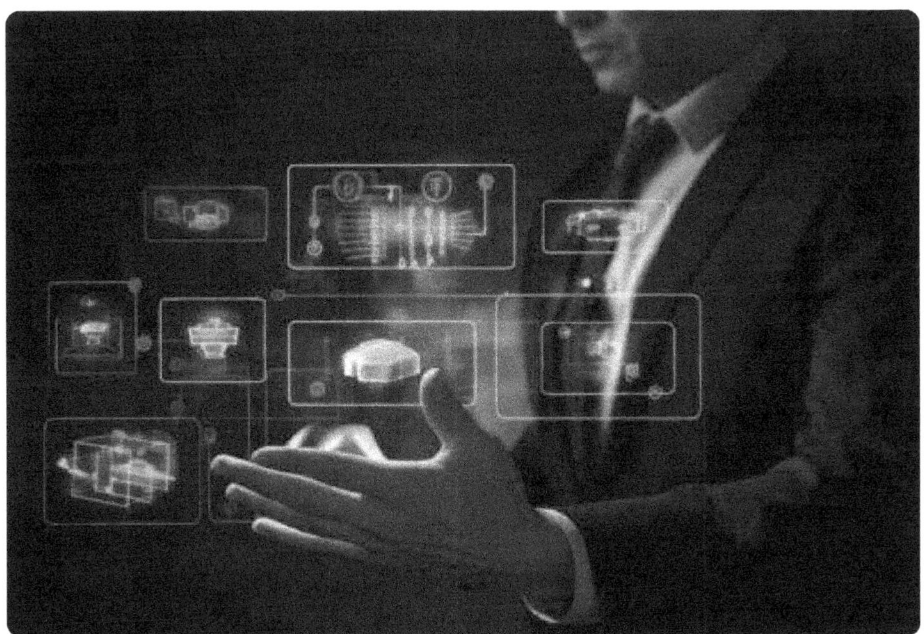

PILLAR 3: CONVERSION AUTOMATION — THE SALES ENGINE

This is the final, critical piece of your AI Customer Acquisition Engine™. Your content and nurture sequences create visibility and trust — but now you need a system to consistently convert warm leads into paying customers.

Your AI-Powered Sales Funnel Structure

Funnel Flow:

1. Lead Magnet:
   Offer a free, valuable resource — a guide, checklist, webinar, or template. (Use AI to create the copy, design, and offer)

2. Nurture Sequence:
   Automatically engage leads with the email sequence from Pillar 2.

3. Sales Page / Offer Page:
   A clear, persuasive landing page explaining the offer. (Use AI to write the sales copy, then refine it with your brand voice)

4. Call-To-Action:
   Encourage your audience to:
   - Book a discovery call
   - Register for a masterclass
   - Purchase directly

5. Follow-Up Automation:
   Send:
   - Reminder emails
   - Abandoned cart recovery
   - Limited-time offers

Prompt Example:

"Write a sales landing page for our AI Customer Acquisition Bootcamp, targeting entrepreneurs and professionals who want to use AI to grow their business. Include key benefits, social proof, pricing, and a strong call-to-action."

PILLAR 3: CONVERSION AUTOMATION — THE SALES ENGINE

Your AI-Powered Sales Funnel Structure

Execution Steps:
1. Create your landing page copy using AI
2. Edit and personalise
3. Build the funnel using platforms like:
   - ClickFunnels
   - Leadpages
   - WordPress + Elementor
4. Integrate payment processors (Stripe, PayPal)
5. Connect confirmation emails and thank-you pages

Outcome:

You now have a fully automated sales system working 24/7 — turning interested leads into paying customers without manual chasing.

ADVANCED STRATEGY: THE AI + AUTOMATION TECH STACK

Here's a recommended tech stack you can implement (or delegate to your team):

PURPOSE	RECOMMENDED TOOLS
AI Content Creation	ChatGPT, Jasper, Copy.ai, Claude, Grok
Email Automation	ActiveCampaign, MailChimp, ConvertKit, HubSpot
Social Media Scheduling	Buffer, Hootsuite, Later
Funnel Building	ClickFunnels, Leadpages, WordPress + Elementor
CRM & Customer Tracking	HubSpot, Zoho CRM, Pipedrive
Payment Integration	Stripe, PayPal, Razorpay
Analytics & Tracking	Google Analytics, Meta Pixel, Hotjar

Start lean.
Build one funnel first.
Then scale.

Your 7-Day AI Customer Acquisition Engine Implementation Plan

DAY TASK

DAY 1	DAY 2	DAY 3	DAY 4	DAY 5	DAY 6	DAY 7
Define your idea customer profile & content objective	Build your AI Prompt Library (see Section 3)	Create your Lead Magnet & Landing Page content with AI	Write a 5–7 email nurture sequence using AI	Set up email automation & content scheduler	Test your funnel, emails, automation, and payment system	Launch. Monitor performance. Refine with AI insights.

When you implement this system, here's what you'll experience:

- Your content will be consistent and strategic
- Your lead generation will run on autopilot
- Your nurture sequence will build trust without your daily involvement
- Your sales funnel will convert without manual chasing
- Your entire customer acquisition process will become predictable, scalable, and sustainable

You will no longer be at the mercy of algorithms, content deadlines, or sales uncertainty.

You'll own a fully operational, AI-powered, human-optimised **Customer Acquisition Engine™.**

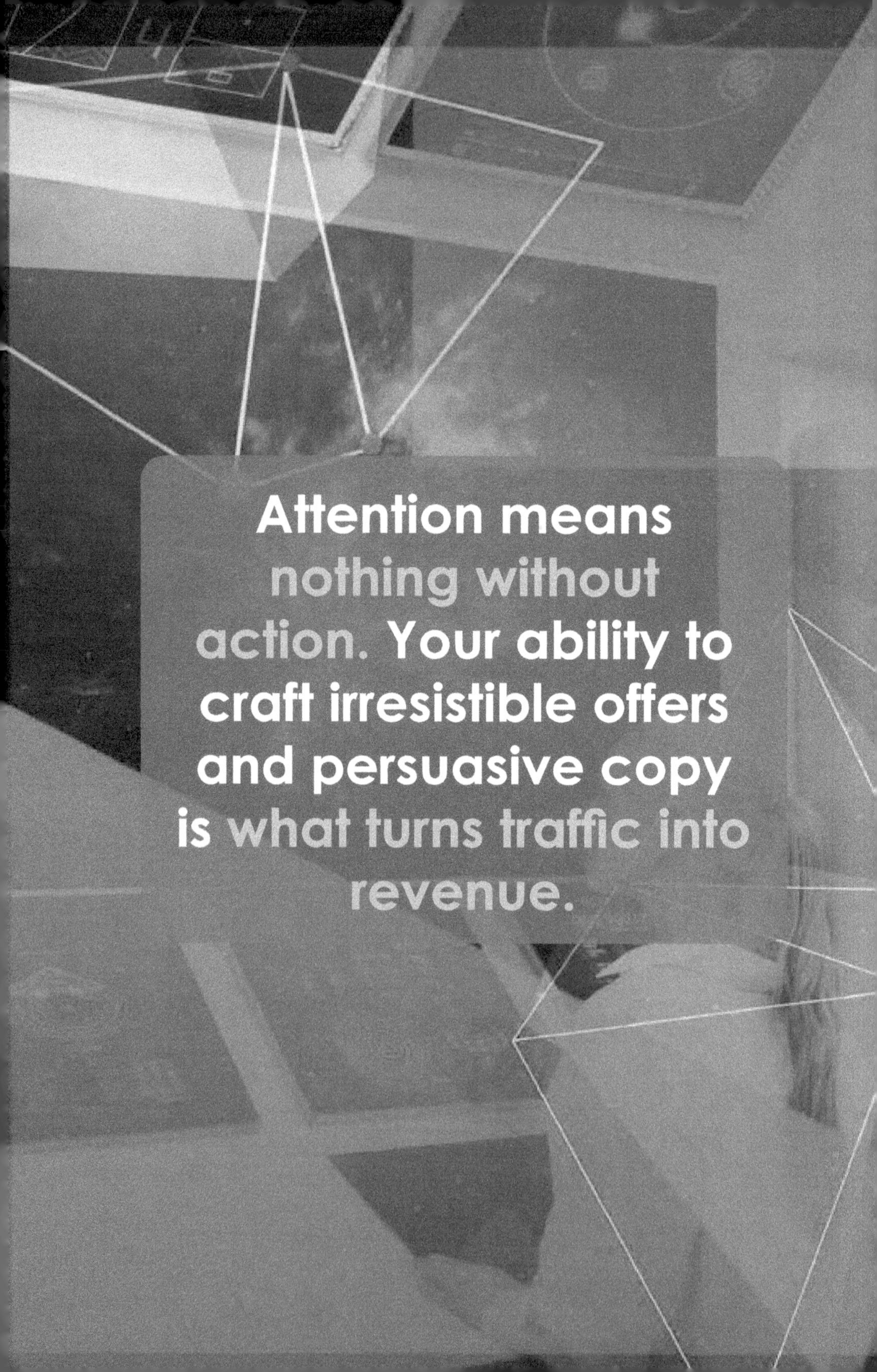
Attention means nothing without action. Your ability to craft irresistible offers and persuasive copy is what turns traffic into revenue.

THE AI SALES CONVERSION BLUEPRINT™ — HOW TO WRITE IRRESISTIBLE OFFERS & SALES COPY THAT CONVERT

THE REAL CHALLENGE OF AI IN SALES

Attracting attention is easy.
Engaging people online is easier than ever with AI.
But turning that attention into actual revenue?
That's where 99% of business owners, entrepreneurs, and marketers fail.
And the reason is simple:

Most AI-generated sales content is:
- Too generic
- Too long-winded and confusing
- Focused on the seller instead of the buyer
- Missing clarity, urgency, and proof
- Sounds robotic, not human

AI can help you create content, but it will not convert customers unless you know how to build powerful, persuasive offers—and structure your sales copy with precision and intent.

This section will show you how to do exactly that.
You'll learn how to make AI your ultimate sales weapon — crafting high-converting copy without sounding like a pushy salesperson, all while keeping your brand voice intact.

What You'll Learn in This Section

- How to design irresistible, high-value offers using AI
- How to structure persuasive sales pages, emails, and scripts
- How to embed proven psychological triggers inside your AI prompts
- How to ethically use urgency, scarcity, and social proof
- How to refine and humanise every AI-generated draft

PART A: START WITH THE OFFER — NOT THE COPY

The biggest mistake people make when writing sales copy is starting with the writing.

But copy is only as good as the offer behind it.

Think of it this way: You can hire the world's best copywriter or use the most advanced AI model — but if your offer is weak, no amount of words will make people buy.

The Irresistible Offer Formula™

Before you write a single word, clarify these seven offer elements:

1	**Core Product/Service** What exactly are you selling?
2	**The Big Promise** What is the #1 transformation, result, or benefit your customer will experience?
3	**Supporting Benefits** What secondary benefits will they enjoy?
4	**Proof & Authority** Why should they trust you? Testimonials, case studies, experience, credentials.
5	**Risk Reversal** What makes the offer risk-free? Guarantee, refund policy, trial.
6	**Scarcity & Urgency** Why should they act now? Limited seats, limited-time bonuses, deadlines.
7	**Clear Call-To-Action** What's the next step you want them to take?

Prompt Example:
"Help me build an irresistible offer for my AI Customer Acquisition Masterclass. The promise is to teach entrepreneurs how to get customers fast using AI. Include key benefits, risk reversal, bonuses, scarcity, and a strong call-to-action."

Once you build a solid offer, the sales copy becomes easy — because you're no longer selling hype. You're presenting real value.

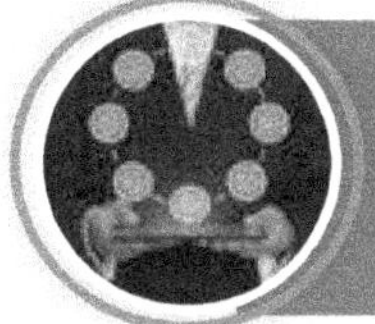

PART B: STRUCTURE YOUR SALES COPY LIKE A PRO

High-converting sales copy follows a formula.

There's a reason why the best copywriters, agencies, and brands all follow proven frameworks — because they work.

The 9-Part Sales Letter Framework™

1	**Headline:** Grab attention with a bold, benefit-driven promise.
2	**Opening Hook or Story:** Connect emotionally. Start with a relatable pain point, aspiration, or story.
3	**The Big Promise & Benefits:** Clearly explain the transformation your audience will experience.
4	**Authority & Proof:** Show why you're credible. Use social proof, results, or credentials.
5	**Explanation:** Explain how your solution works — simply, clearly, and logically.
6	**Offer & Bonuses:** List exactly what they get when they buy, including bonuses.
7	**Risk Reversal:** Remove the fear of buying. Include a money-back guarantee or no-obligation trial.
8	**Urgency & Scarcity:** Create a genuine reason to act now.
9	**Clear Call-To-Action:** Tell them exactly what to do next.

Prompt Example:

"Write a long-form sales page for our AI Customer Acquisition Bootcamp using the 9-Part Sales Letter Framework. The audience is entrepreneurs aged 30–50 who want to grow their business using AI. Use a professional, persuasive, and conversational tone."

Once AI generates the draft, review, personalise, and refine.

The goal is to sound human, credible, and compelling.

PART C: EMBED PERSUASION PSYCHOLOGY INTO YOUR AI CONTENT

Good sales copy is not about fancy words — it's about human psychology.

You can (and should) embed psychological triggers directly into your AI prompts.

The 6 Universal Principles of Persuasion

1	**Reciprocity:** Give value before asking for the sale. --> Use free resources, insights, tips.
2	**Authority:** Showcase credibility and expertise. --> Share case studies, testimonials, credentials.
3	**Social Proof:** Demonstrate that others trust you. --> Highlight client stories, media features.
4	**Scarcity:** Create urgency and exclusivity. --> Limited seats, bonuses, or deadlines.
5	**Consistency:** Align your offer with your audience's goals, values, and previous actions.
6	**Liking:** Be relatable and trustworthy. --> Write in a friendly, helpful, conversational tone.

Prompt Example:
"Revise this sales letter to incorporate social proof, risk reversal, and urgency without sounding aggressive. Keep the tone professional, helpful, and trustworthy."

When you combine these triggers with the right AI structure, your conversion rates will increase dramatically.

PART D: ACTIVATE BEAST MODE — THE COPY REFINEMENT PROCESS

Once AI generates your sales copy, you're only halfway done.
The difference between good copy and great copy is in the refinement.

Here's how to activate Beast Mode™ and make your sales copy elite:

Step 1: Review for Flow & Voice
Prompt: *"Revise this sales letter to match my brand voice — professional, direct, conversational, no jargon."*
Step 2: Simplify & Clarify
Prompt: *"Rewrite this draft at a Grade 6 reading level. Shorten sentences. Remove fluff. Make the message clearer and more impactful."*
Step 3: Strengthen The Headlines
Prompt: *"Give me 10 hard-hitting, curiosity-driven headlines for this sales letter. Make them bold, benefit-focused, and irresistible."*   **Example Outputs:**   • "Unlock 10x Business Growth with AI (Without Hiring More Staff)"   • "The AI Customer Growth Formula Nobody Taught You"   • "How To Get More Customers in 30 Days — Powered by AI"
Step 4: Strengthen The Call-To-Action
Prompt: *"Revise the final call-to-action to make it stronger, clearer, and more urgent — without sounding aggressive."*

This process will elevate every piece of AI-generated sales content — and make it sound human, powerful, and persuasive.

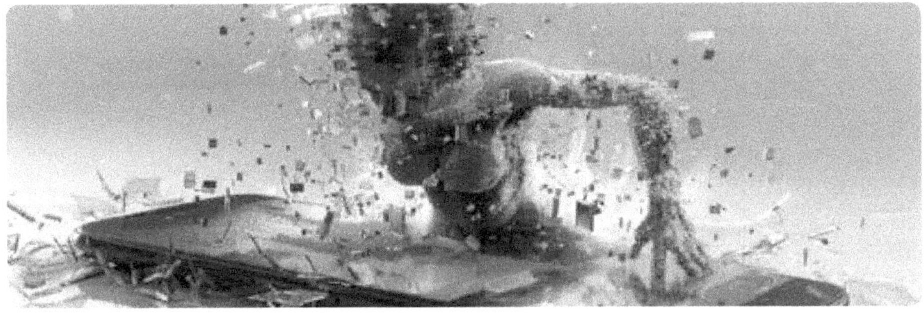

PART E: QUICK WIN SALES COPY TEMPLATES

Here are pre-built AI prompt templates you can start using immediately:

Sales Email Prompt:
"Write a persuasive sales email introducing our 'AI Customer Acquisition Bootcamp' to entrepreneurs aged 25–40. Highlight the key benefits, include a client testimonial, and end with a strong call-to-action."
Webinar Invitation Prompt:
"Write a professional email inviting professionals to attend our free webinar 'How to Get Customers Fast Using AI.' Include three key benefits and a clear call-to-action to register."
Offer Email with Scarcity:
"Write an email announcing the final 24 hours to register for our AI Customer Acquisition Masterclass. Create urgency, remind them of the key benefits, include risk reversal, and a clear call-to-action."
Limited Time Bonus Prompt:
"Write an email announcing an exclusive bonus for the first 20 people who join our AI Growth Bootcamp. Make it exciting, urgent, and highlight why they should act now."

Action Plan — Craft & Launch Your Sales Copy Today

Here's how to implement what you've just learned:
1. Outline your irresistible offer using the Offer Formula.
2. Structure your sales message using the 9-Part Sales Letter Framework.
3. Use AI to draft your sales copy — then run it through Beast Mode™ Refinement.
4. Polish, personalise, and embed persuasion triggers.
5. Load your copy into your sales funnel and automation system.

You now have professional, persuasive, brand-aligned sales content — created at scale, in minutes.

THE BIG PICTURE

By the time you complete this step, you will not just have great content.
You will have a fully structured, conversion-ready, AI-powered **Customer Acquisition System™ — infused with strategy, persuasion, and your authentic voice.**

In the next and final section (Section 6), I will show you how to tie everything together — with a clear roadmap, recommended next steps, and advanced strategies to continue scaling your AI-powered growth engine.

____

____

____

____

____

____

____

____

____

____

____

____

____

____

____

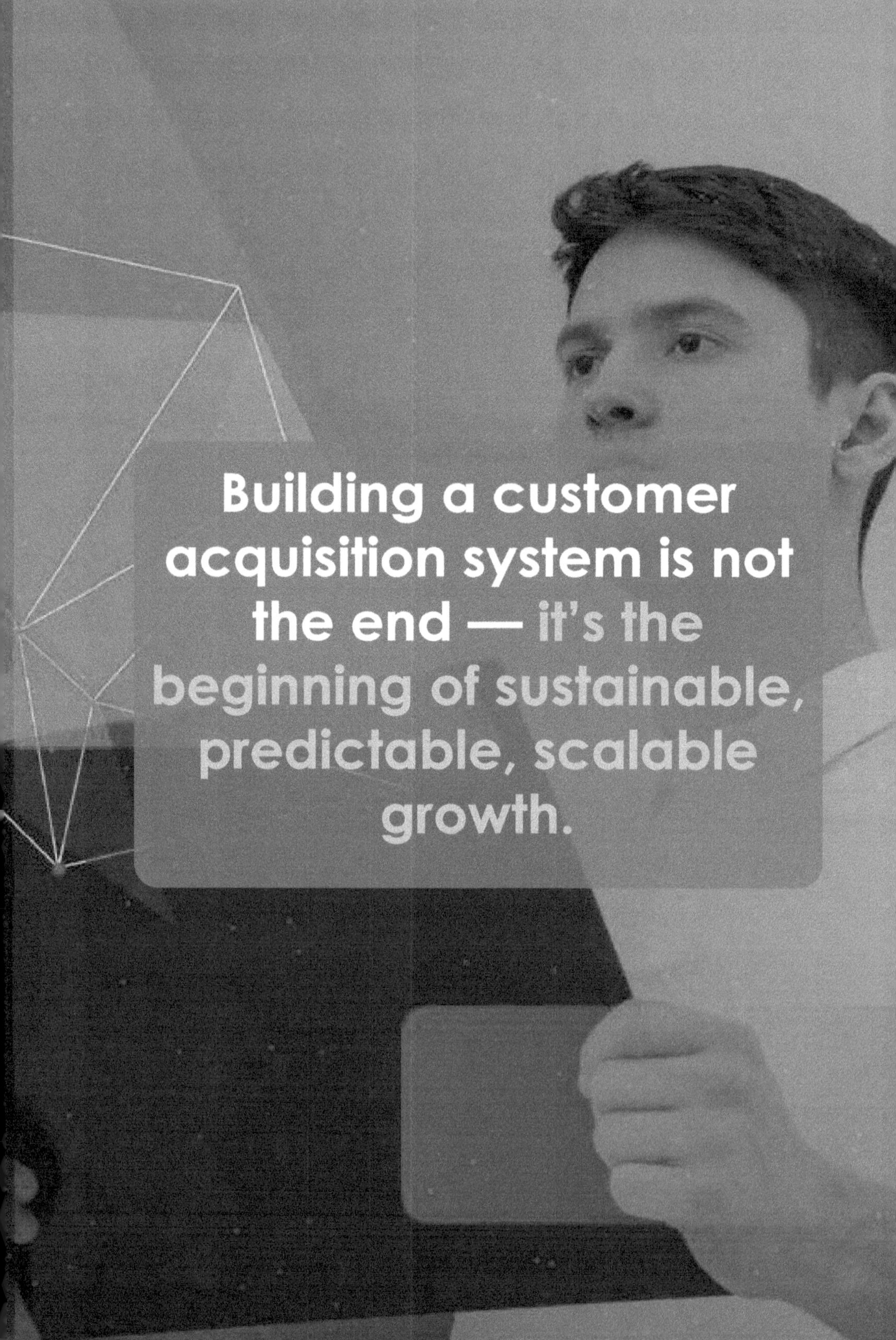
Building a customer acquisition system is not the end — it's the beginning of sustainable, predictable, scalable growth.

THE SCALING BLUEPRINT™ — YOUR NEXT STEPS TO SUSTAINABLE AI-POWERED GROWTH

YOU'VE BUILT THE ENGINE. NOW IT'S TIME TO SCALE

By now, you've done what 99% of entrepreneurs, executives, and sales professionals never do.

- You've moved beyond the AI hype.
- You've learned how to use AI strategically, not randomly.
- You've created clear systems to attract, nurture, and convert customers — without burning out.

But this isn't the finish line.
This is just the beginning.

The real power of AI lies not in creating content...
...but in creating predictable, scalable, and sustainable customer acquisition systems.

This final section is your blueprint to keep building, growing, and scaling — without adding more hours to your day.

What You'll Learn in This Section
- How to review and refine your AI acquisition system
- How to add advanced AI strategies for scale
- How to avoid the common scaling mistakes
- How to future-proof your brand in the AI age
- The next-level programs and resources to deepen your mastery

PART A: REVIEW, REFINE & OPTIMISE

Your first version is never your final version.
The biggest brands and marketers constantly refine.
You must too.

Here's how to review and strengthen your system:

1. Audit Your Customer Acquisition Funnel

- Is every piece of content aligned with your audience's pain points and goals?
- Is your nurture sequence clear, value-driven, and persuasive?
- Is your sales offer irresistible and easy to act on?

2. Track Key Metrics

You can't improve what you don't measure.
Track:
- Lead conversion rate
- Email open & click rates
- Sales funnel drop-off points
- Customer acquisition cost

3. Use AI Insights for Optimisation

Prompt Example:
"Review the following email sequence and suggest three ways to make it more persuasive, engaging, and clear."

Refinement is where the long-term wins are made.
The more you review and optimise, the faster you'll grow — sustainably.

PART B: ADD ADVANCED AI STRATEGIES

Once your core engine is running, you can start adding advanced AI strategies to multiply your impact:

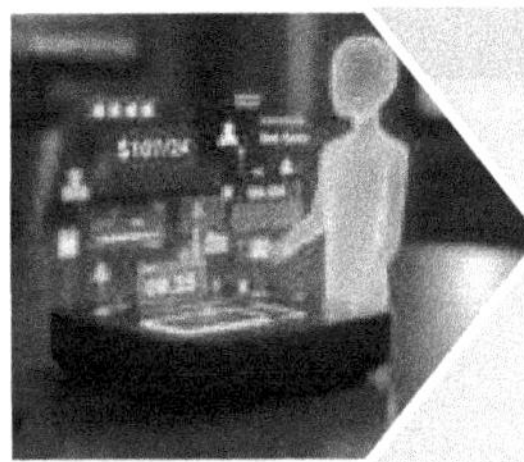

1. AI-Driven Personalisation at Scale

Use AI to customise your content based on specific audience segments.

Example: *"Write two versions of this email — one for financial advisors under 35, and one for corporate leaders over 45. Tailor the tone and examples."*

2. Content Repurposing

One sales letter can become:
- 5 LinkedIn posts
- 3 email newsletters
- 1 lead magnet
- 1 webinar script

Prompt Example:
"Repurpose this sales page into a 5-part LinkedIn content series, keeping the same core message but adjusting for social media."

3. AI-Powered Customer Journey Mapping

Use AI to help you map and design the entire customer experience:
- From first touchpoint to sale
- From onboarding to repeat purchase

Prompt Example: *"Based on this product, design a full customer journey touchpoint map — including content ideas for each stage."*

This is how you move from content creator to growth strategist.

PART C: AVOID THESE COMMON SCALING MISTAKES

When scaling your AI system, most people fall into one of three traps:

Mistake 1: Over-Automation Without Connection

Automating everything without human touch leads to cold, robotic customer experiences.

Always leave space for human conversations and real engagement.

Mistake 2: Scaling Too Soon

Many entrepreneurs try to scale before their funnel is tested and optimised.

**Focus first on conversion rates.
Then add automation and scale.**

Mistake 3: Ignoring Brand Consistency

The more content you publish, the more important your voice becomes.

Always ensure AI-generated content matches your brand's personality and values.

PART D: FUTURE-PROOF YOUR BUSINESS IN THE AGE OF AI

AI is evolving — fast.
But the principles you've learned in this playbook will outlast any new platform or algorithm.

Here's what will never change:

- **The need for clear strategy**
- **The power of human connection**
- **The importance of persuasive, brand-driven communication**

When you combine these timeless principles with cutting-edge AI tools, you will always stay ahead of the curve.

PART E: YOUR NEXT-LEVEL GROWTH PLAN

If you want to take your AI-powered customer acquisition system even further, here's what I recommend:

1. Complete Your AI Execution Checklist

Review your progress:
- Have you built your Brand Voice Template?
- Have you created your Prompt Library?
- Is your full funnel automated and tested?
- Have you refined your sales copy using the Beast Mode™ process?

If not — go back, complete it, and strengthen your foundation.

2. Enrol in Advanced Programs

To continue mastering AI-driven growth, here are the next-level programs and workshops I recommend:
- **The AI Customer Acquisition Masterclass™**
  A 2-hour deep dive into advanced AI strategies, content funnels, and persuasive copy frameworks.
- **The AI Sales Conversion Bootcamp™**
  A hands-on program to help you build, launch, and optimise your AI-powered sales funnel — in real-time.
- **The AI Growth Accelerator™ (Premium Program)**
  A full-scale coaching program for entrepreneurs and businesses who want to scale their AI systems, optimise marketing, and grow revenue sustainably.

2. Build an AI-Optimised Brand Ecosystem

This playbook is focused on customer acquisition — but AI can (and should) touch every part of your brand ecosystem:
- Customer Service
- Content Marketing
- Sales Automation
- Personal Branding
- Internal Communication
- Product Development

The future belongs to those who build AI-enhanced, human-led brands.

YOUR FINAL ACTION PLAN

TASK	OUTCOME
Review & optimise your current funnel	Improve performance and conversion rates
Apply advanced AI strategies (personalisation, repurposing)	Scale visibility and engagement
Avoid over-automation and maintain human connection	Protect your brand trust and credibility
Continue learning through advanced programs	Future-proof your skills and business growth
Build an AI-optimised business ecosystem	Unlock exponential growth potential

THE BIG PICTURE

You've now gone beyond theory.
You've built something powerful — an AI-powered, automated, scalable **Customer Acquisition Engine™.**

But the real win isn't the automation.
It's that you've built a system that:
- Attracts your ideal customers
- Nurtures relationships at scale
- Converts leads predictably
- Grows with or without you

You are no longer at the mercy of the algorithm, market noise, or inconsistent sales.
You now control your customer flow — powered by AI, fuelled by strategy, and led by your brand.

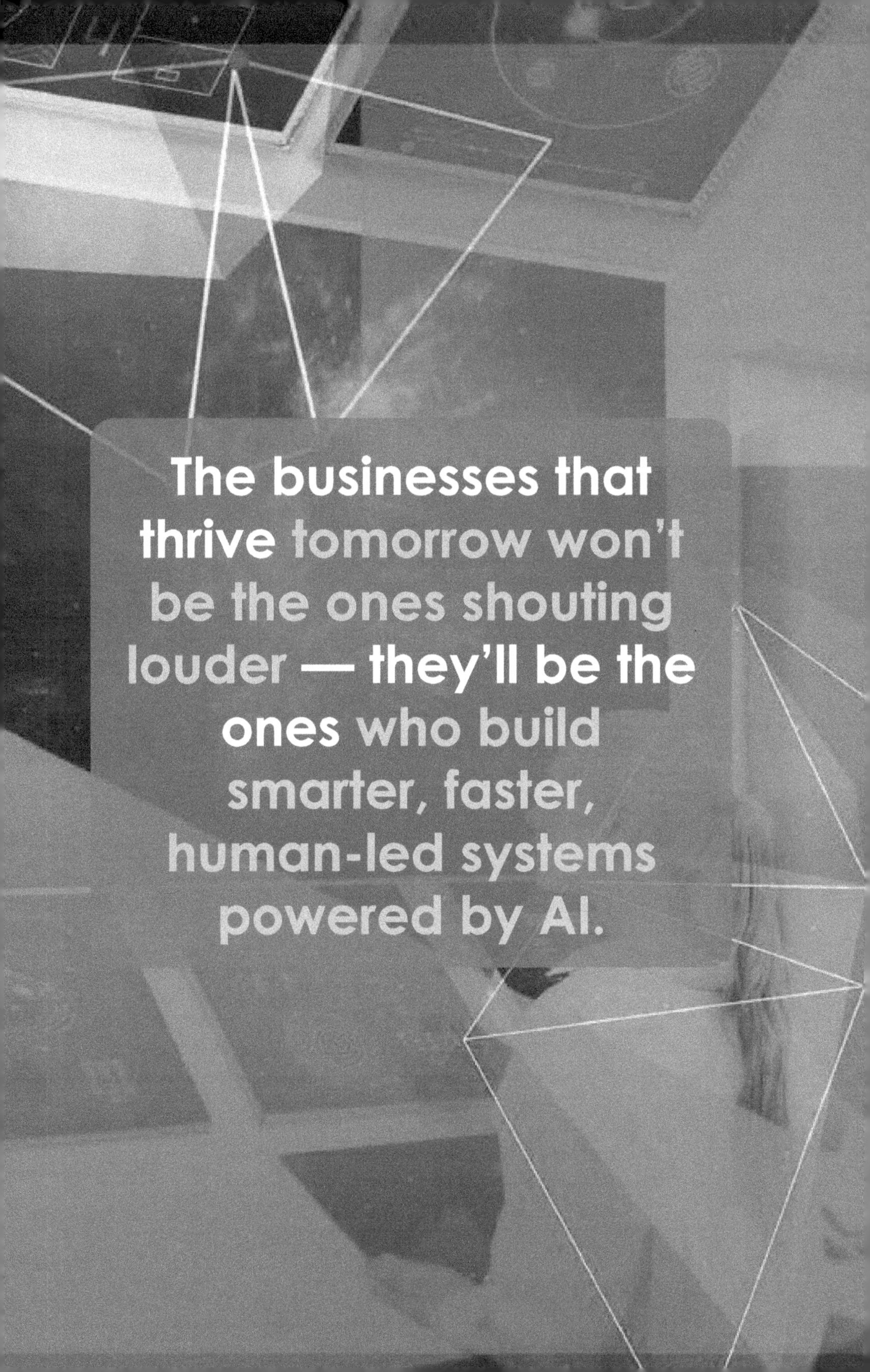

The businesses that thrive tomorrow won't be the ones shouting louder — they'll be the ones who build smarter, faster, human-led systems powered by AI.

The Future of Customer Acquisition is in Your Hands

You've reached the end of this playbook — but in reality, this is the beginning of something far more powerful.

In a world where AI has become the most disruptive force in marketing, sales, and business growth, most people are still stuck on the surface:
- Chasing hacks and gimmicks
- Drowning in content chaos
- Treating AI like a toy instead of a tool

You are now different.
You've done what few ever do:
- You've learned the real strategy behind AI-powered customer acquisition
- You've built a system, not just content
- You've mastered how to attract, nurture, and convert customers — at scale

You now possess something far more valuable than tools or tactics: You have the mindset, framework, and system to create predictable, sustainable business growth — powered by AI and led by you.

What You've Achieved

In this playbook, you've learned how to:
- Avoid the common traps and mistakes of AI usage
- Build powerful, persuasive offers that resonate
- Engineer high-converting sales copy and funnels
- Automate your entire customer acquisition process
- Scale sustainably without sacrificing authenticity or connection

You haven't just learned how to use AI.
You've learned how to turn AI into a strategic growth engine — one that works even when you're not.

YOUR NEXT MOVE

Knowledge without action is meaningless.
So here's what I want you to do next:

1. Review your notes and key action steps.
Make sure you've completed each part of your Customer Acquisition Engine™.

2. Launch. Test. Refine.
Start with one offer, one funnel, one audience.
Test it. Track your results. Improve.

3. Join the next-level programs.
If you want to deepen your mastery, I invite you to join the AI Customer Acquisition Masterclass™ or the AI Growth Accelerator™ — where I'll help you build, scale, and optimise your system live.

4. Future-proof your brand.
AI will evolve. Tools will change. Algorithms will shift.
But what will always remain is the need for strategic, human-led, ethical marketing systems.

You now have the blueprint.
The next chapter is yours to write.

A FINAL WORD

The businesses that will dominate the next decade won't be the ones shouting the loudest.
They'll be the ones who show up strategically, consistently, and authentically—backed by systems, supported by technology, and driven by human connection.
You now have everything you need to become one of them.

Your future customers are waiting.
Your growth engine is ready.
The next move is yours.

Your brand, your business, and your future will not be defined by technology — but by how you lead, connect, and grow in the age of technology.

Dr. Jerome Joseph & The Signature AI Customer Acquisition System™

WHO IS DR. JEROME JOSEPH?

Dr. Jerome Joseph, CSP, GSF, PMC, is recognised globally as a leading authority in Branding, Sales Growth, and Business Strategy — with a specialised focus on helping leaders, entrepreneurs, and organisations scale using real-world, actionable systems.

With over 28 years of global experience, Dr. Jerome has:

- Worked with over 1,000 brands across 38 countries
- Authored 10 best-selling books on Branding, Sales, and Leadership
- Delivered impactful programs to over 12,000 leaders and entrepreneurs annually
- Been ranked No. 2 Global Brand Thought Leader in the world (2020 & 2022)
- Served as CEO & Board Member of a publicly-listed brand agency
- Inducted into the Asia Speaker Hall of Fame for lifetime contribution to professional speaking

But beyond the accolades and global recognition, Dr. Jerome's mission is clear: To empower business leaders to amplify their visibility, authority, and growth — strategically, sustainably, and ethically. He believes that AI is not here to replace you. It's here to multiply your results — if you know how to use it the right way. Reach out to Dr. Jerome Joseph:

Website: www.jeromejoseph.com
Email: jerome@jeromejoseph.com

The Signature AI Customer Acquisition System™

After years of consulting, training, and speaking to business leaders across the world, Dr. Jerome saw a growing problem:
Entrepreneurs and professionals were being drowned in AI hype…
but lacked a structured, ethical, strategic system to actually turn AI into business growth.
That's why he created the AI Customer Acquisition System™ — a proven, step-by-step framework to help leaders, entrepreneurs, and sales professionals attract, nurture, and convert customers at scale.

The System Includes 6 Core Pillars:

1. Clarity Before Technology

You cannot automate what you haven't defined.
This pillar ensures you start with clear business objectives, audience targeting, and brand voice.

2. Mastering Prompt Engineering

Your AI output is only as powerful as your input.
You'll learn how to create high-quality, strategic prompts that generate persuasive, human-sounding content.

3. The Rewrite & Amplify System™

Using AI to transform underperforming, boring, or outdated content into brand-driven, high-converting assets.

4. The Voice Calibration Method™

Training AI to speak exactly like you — preserving your brand personality, values, and authority at scale.

5. The Sales Conversion Blueprint™

A step-by-step structure to build irresistible offers, write high-converting sales copy, and embed psychological triggers ethically.

6. The Automation & Scaling Blueprint™

Training AI to speak exactly like you — preserving your brand personality, values, and authority at scale.

Why This System Matters

This isn't another generic how-to-AI guide.
The AI Customer Acquisition System™ is designed to give you:

- A strategic edge in an increasingly competitive digital marketplace
- A replicable, scalable model that works across industries
- A human-led, brand-driven approach to AI-powered growth
- The ability to systemise your marketing and sales without losing authenticity

Whether you're an entrepreneur, executive, sales leader, or marketing professional — this playbook and the system within it will empower you to stop guessing, start growing, and lead in the new digital age.

CONNECT WITH US:

The Global Brand Academy
www.globalbrandacademy.com
business@globalbrandacademy.com

The Global Brand Academy is a premier training and consulting firm that transforms brands through high-impact programs in Branding, Sales, Leadership, Culture, and AI.

Dr. Jerome Joseph
www.jeromejoseph.com
jerome@jeromejoseph.com

Signature Programs by Dr. Jerome Joseph:
Personal Branding in the Age of AI
Sell the Brand: Sales Mastery & Social Selling
Digital Branding Mastery
AI-Driven Marketing
Creating a Brand-Driven Culture
The Future of Work in the Age of AI
Purpose-Driven Leadership for the Future
Customer Acquisition System
Sales Mastery System

Follow Dr. Jerome Joseph Online:

Instagram   Facebook   LinkedIn   YouTube   TikTok

www.ingramcontent.com/pod-product-compliance
Lightning Source LLC
Chambersburg PA
CBHW040109150726
48005CB00013B/1627